Chapter 1
Science Fair Time

Katy Beth Allen sat behind Jeremy Walker that morning in assembly. Jeremy was very quiet and very clever. Sometimes, in class, Katy Beth peeked to see what grade he made on his test. He always got an A. Or she peeked to see what he wrote about in his journal. He always wrote the longest entries of anyone in the class. Or she peeked to see what book he was reading. He liked to read about the solar system and tornadoes. Katy Beth thought that Jeremy Walker was the smartest boy in the whole class.

"I bet I know how to spell all the words on the spelling pretest today," Maya whispered to Katy Beth. Maya was Katy Beth's best friend. Katy Beth opened her eyes. She'd been daydreaming about the vacation she and her family were planning for spring break. They were going to visit Yellowstone National Park in Wyoming.

Katy Beth didn't have a chance to whisper anything to Maya. It was time to stand up.

The voices rang out, "I pledge allegiance… with liberty and justice for all!"

"And now for the announcements." It was Mr. Guzman, the principal. He had a loud voice that echoed through the assembly hall. Katy Beth imagined him up in the announcer's booth of the town's stadium during baseball season. There, he would name the players for the Little League ball games. He seemed to think about baseball all the time.

"On March 20, Clarence Elementary School will hold its annual Science Fair," he boomed. "That's six weeks from now, the week after spring break. Get busy and good luck! Make every inning count!"

Katy Beth smiled. *There he goes again. He has baseball on the brain,* she thought.

A Science Fair! Wow! Katy Beth closed her eyes and imagined herself in a white coat, the kind scientists wear. That's what she wanted to be when she grew up—a scientist. And she knew exactly what she wanted to do for her project.

Katy Beth would build a volcano. She had read about volcanoes once in a library book of science experiments. Her volcano would be the biggest and best! It would bubble, erupt, and ooze. How cool! She knew just how she would do it. She would form the volcano from clay. She would put a little cup just below the opening at the top.

Katy Beth couldn't wait! She would put baking soda and red food coloring in the cup. Then she would add vinegar. Boom! Lava would fizz up and pour down the volcano as it erupted.

Chapter 2
Making Plans

Miss Einstein picked up her class in the gym. They walked back to the classroom.

"So you have six weeks to prepare your Science Fair projects," Miss Einstein said as the class settled in. "Let's take about a week to think about our projects. We'll go to the library to help you get some ideas. We can make this year's fair the best ever. I know you can do it!" said Miss Einstein. She *always* said, "I know you can do it!"

True to her word, later in the week Miss Einstein took the class to the library. The library had a lot of books about Science Fair projects.

Maya read a book on bugs carefully. "This sounds interesting," Maya whispered. "You tattoo insects and track their travels." Maya liked bugs. When Katy Beth and Maya were outdoors, Katy Beth always had to remind her friend not to pick up bugs.

"Mmmhmm," Katy Beth answered. But she wasn't really listening. She was planning her volcano. It would be the biggest and best volcano in the universe. It would spit out red volcanic lava, and everyone would be scared. In fact, she wouldn't tell anyone about the volcano until the day of the fair. It would be a surprise. She looked at Jeremy, sitting quietly with his book. She imagined how surprised and amazed Jeremy would be when he saw her volcano erupt.

As the week went by, Katy Beth thought about her volcano. She drew up her plans, but she kept them secret, hiding them in her room at home. She was trying to come up with a way to add sound effects.

But sometimes Katy Beth thought about things other than her volcano. She thought about her family's trip to Yellowstone National Park. It was exciting to imagine what she'd see there. Katy Beth couldn't wait. She was looking forward to the trip as much as making her volcano.

On Monday, Miss Einstein said, "Now, that you've had some time to think about your science projects, let's hear your ideas. Maya?"

Maya said, "I'm going to show how bugs travel."

Miss Einstein said, "I know you can do it."

Jeremy's hand shot up. "I will build an erupting volcano," he said proudly.

"Oh, how exciting!" said Miss Einstein. "I know you can do it! And what will you do, Katy Beth?"

Oh, no! thought Katy Beth. *I can't believe that Jeremy is making a volcano! I didn't tell anyone about my idea, not even Maya. Now what will I do?*

"Well," said Katy Beth. She couldn't actually say that she'd thought of a volcano, too. It would be too embarrassing. "My project is… it's about… it's about…." She looked out at the rain streaking down the windows. "It's about water and…." Her voice trailed off.

Miss Einstein nodded and said, "That's interesting…."

Chapter 3

Water, Water Everywhere

One day, Katy Beth and Maya were walking home from school. Maya was talking about her bug experiment. Suddenly, a butterfly came down and fluttered its wings. Maya cried, "Look, Katy Beth!" Maya ran after the butterfly, and Katy Beth ran after Maya.

"I wish I could catch that butterfly," called Maya.

But the faster Maya and Katy Beth ran, the faster the butterfly flew, until it flew out of sight.

"Oh, well," said Maya. "That would have been great for my science experiment. But now I'm thirsty. Let's get some water."

"Water! I'm sick of water. I wish I hadn't told Miss Einstein that I'd do my project about water. It's boring. *B O R I N G !* I'd much rather build a volcano," said Katy Beth.

Later, Katy Beth thought about water as she wrote in her journal.

Dear Journal,

Water, water. I read once in a book that the human body is almost three-fourths water. We need to drink a lot of water. We need about two quarts each day. It can come in our food or just as plain water. So what? Well, maybe my project can be a water taste test. I could have different kinds of bottled water for people to sample. You don't usually get to eat or drink someone's Science Fair project. But it might be kind of neat. I'll think about it. What else could I do with water?

BOOM

3/4
WATER

As the Science Fair inched closer, Maya tracked bugs, and Katy Beth thought about water.

One rainy day, Miss Einstein said they could work on their projects since there was no recess. Out of the corner of her eye, Katy Beth watched Jeremy. He had brought a large square wooden board to school. He was beginning to build his volcano with pieces of paper dipped in flour paste.

Katy Beth sighed. She tried to think about water. But her mind kept wandering. Jeremy was still busy with his volcano. Katy Beth tried not to notice. Instead, she thought about her vacation and watched the rain fall outside. Then she took out her journal and began to write.

Dear Journal,

It's raining. How many times have those drops fallen from the sky? All the water on Earth has been here forever. It just gets used over again. It seems to disappear. But it really goes back into the air and the clouds. When they get heavy, the water falls back to Earth.

Last week, I put two jars of water outside. I covered one jar with foil. I left the other jar open. This morning, I checked them. The water disappeared much faster in the open jar. That's evaporation.

How can I make a project out of evaporation? I'd have to call it Invisible Water. I'm wishing my project wasn't on water!

Water evaporates.

Rain falls.

At home, Katy Beth talked to her parents about her project.

"We can't do without water," Dad said.

"Yes, and where would fish live?" Mom teased.

"Did you know that of all the water on Earth, we can only use a tiny bit of what there is? Most of the water is salty," Katy Beth explained.

"That's true," said Dad. "Maybe you could do an experiment with salt water!"

"That might be more special than a volcano," said Katy Beth.

"Let's do an experiment together, right now," said Dad.

Later, Katy Beth wrote about the experiment in her journal.

Dear Journal,

Dad and I did an experiment to take salt out of water. We put water and salt into a small pan. First, we tasted the salt water. **YUCK!** 😫 Then we heated it. When it boiled, Dad put a lid on the pan. Then he took the lid off and dripped the drops of water from it into a cup. We had to do it several times to get enough water. After it cooled, we had a little taste. The water didn't taste salty any more! The salt stayed behind in the pan.

This is a good experiment! But I can't boil water in the gym. No, I'll have to think of something else. Water, water, water. What can I do with water?

Katy Beth was getting worried. After all, she had only three weeks until it was Science Fair day. And she still hadn't decided on what experiment to do with water.

One day, Katy Beth's mom took her and Maya to the park. They stopped to look at the pond.

"Hey, I can see myself," Katy Beth said.

"Yes, water can reflect almost like a mirror," Mom explained.

"I wonder if there are any bugs living in there?" asked Maya.

"As a matter of fact, there are! Some bugs you can see, and some you can't. Why don't you take some of this water to school tomorrow and look at it under the microscope," said Mom.

Dear Journal,

Miss Einstein helped us look at the pond water under the microscope. It was great! There were tiny bugs moving all around in the water. Miss Einstein says they are called larvae. That means they're still very young. The pond is their home. Water Bugs You Can't Even See. That could be the name of my project.

But Maya is already doing a bug project. I guess it's back to the drawing board for me. But you know, larvae is one COOL thing about pond water!

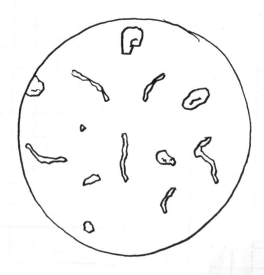

Chapter 4
Inspired!

The Science Fair was getting closer by the day. Mr. Guzman brought it up in morning assembly. "Who has finished their science project?" he asked.

Jeremy and a few others raised their hand.

"Now those of you who aren't finished, let's step up to bat. Get this game going!" he said.

Katy Beth had some ideas about her water project. But nothing excited her as much as the volcano once had.

In fact, she was more excited about her family's trip to Yellowstone Park. They would be going next week—just one week before the fair.

The next time the class went to the library, Katy Beth didn't want to read about water. Then she saw a book about Yellowstone Park. She picked it up and began reading.

Oh, no! Katy Beth thought. *Volcanic activity in Yellowstone Park! Wouldn't you know? I can't get away from volcanoes, even on vacation. Maybe Jeremy should be going to Yellowstone Park!*

Yellowstone National Park

Yellowstone was the first national park. It covers over 3,400 square miles. Most of the park sits in the Rocky Mountains. This is a special part of the mountains, built up by volcanic activity.

Katy Beth read more. She read that many kinds of trees and animals live in the park. Then she read something and stopped. She couldn't believe her eyes.

"This is IT! I'VE GOT IT!" she said loudly.

The librarian raised her eyebrows.

"Sorry!" she whispered. "Miss Einstein, I've got an idea for my project!"

When Katy Beth got home, she set to work. She gathered jars, bowls, and bottles. She dug in the pantry for food coloring. She asked her mom to buy cone-shaped cups. She found an ice chest in the garage, along with flashlights. She checked the batteries. She found clear blue plastic wrap.

Katy Beth went back to the library. She checked out several books. She found what she needed. She wrote these facts on posters. She checked her facts again.

Katy Beth was ready. Her ideas came tumbling out as she wrote in her journal.

Dear Journal,

I've learned so much about water. I can't wait for the fair. I can't wait to surprise everyone!

Who would have thought that I would get my great idea because of our vacation? It will be so exciting to see the real thing at Yellowstone.

Water is <u>Awesome</u>!

Chapter 5
The Surprise

On March 20, Science Fair day, Katy Beth's mom drove her to school. Katy Beth couldn't carry all the stuff she would need.

"What time will you show your experiment?" asked Mom.

"It will be this afternoon. First, all the students set up their projects in the gym," Katy Beth explained. "Then, later, each class goes in to show the judges their projects. Then everyone walks through and looks at all the projects. Parents can come after school or this evening."

"Your dad and I will be there," Mom said. "We can't wait. We are very proud of you, Katy Beth. You didn't get your first choice, but you didn't give up. Now you have a great surprise."

Katy Beth had to agree. She smiled.

Inside the gym, students were setting up their experiments. One student had taped together six plastic mirrors. He was setting up a poster that said, *See Yourself in a Kaleidoscope*. Another student had made a model of the solar system with wire and painted balls. Her poster said, *Our Sun and Our Neighbors*. And another student had put wires into a potato. *Potato Battery Lights Up the Sky*, said the poster.

Maya began to set up her bug experiment. First, she took out a clear, plastic jar with tattooed bugs sitting at the bottom. Then, she put up her posters with maps and bug facts.

At the same time, Jeremy set up his volcano. He knew it was going to be really cool. The volcano would ooze and erupt. Jeremy was sure it would win first prize. He was so excited. He made sure everything was in place. Yes, his volcano was ready to go.

Katy Beth set up her secret experiment. Jeremy and Maya tried to peek, but they couldn't see what she was doing. Katy Beth couldn't wait! *Jeremy would be so surprised. He hadn't seen anything yet. Wait until the judges see this. Everyone will love water,* thought Katy Beth.

After a long morning, it was finally time for Miss Einstein's class to talk to the judges.

On the way to the gym, Miss Einstein reminded her students how proud she was of them. And can you guess what else she said? "I know you can do it!"

They saw Mr. Guzman. He said, "May you all have home runs!"

Maya gave her talk first. She showed the judges her tattooed bugs. She had used books to find out what kinds of bugs they were. She explained what they did and where they lived. She showed the maps she had drawn of where the bugs traveled. Maya was very proud of her bugs.

Other students showed off their experiments. The judges put the kaleidoscope mirror over their heads and saw their faces multiplied a thousand times. Then, they watched the potato battery light up a light bulb. Everyone listened. All of the experiments were interesting.

Soon, it was Jeremy's turn. Katy Beth whispered, "Good luck." He smiled.

Jeremy talked about volcanoes using his fact poster. Then he put baking soda and red and orange food coloring into the volcano. He added the vinegar. The mixture bubbled and streamed down the side. The volcano was *ERUPTING!* Lava flowed up through the vent and out over the sides! The judges asked to see it again. As the lava flowed, students and grownups alike said, "Wow!" and "Ahh!"

29

Finally, Miss Einstein called on Katy Beth. She took her place in front of her experiment. Katy Beth asked Maya to be her assistant. Katy Beth pulled back the covers. The banner read, *Water World!*

"Did you know that the human body is made up of almost three-fourths water?" Katy Beth began. "A person has to drink about two quarts each day to stay healthy. Test the taste of these different brands of bottled water. Don't worry. You won't float away."

Everyone chuckled.

"Water comes in three states of matter—solid, liquid, and gas," Katy Beth went on. "If you add some ice here when you do the taste test, you'll get to enjoy water in two of its states."

Katy Beth was on a roll now. She pointed to a bowl filled with water. "Water is transparent, so we can see through it. But it can also reflect images, like a mirror. Take a peek at yourself in here," she said.

Everyone crowded around to look into the reflecting bowl.

"Water is also the home of millions of animals," Katy Beth said. "Use this microscope to look at tiny bugs that live in pond water."

One by one, students and judges looked into the microscope. "Amazing!" said one. "Oooh!" said another.

Katy Beth moved to the end of the table. Miss Einstein walked up carrying a small bottle with an oven mitt.

"And now, at last," said Katy Beth, "I will present you with the true wonder of Water World!"

Katy Beth opened the small bottle and poured in blue food coloring. "This is hot water. The color will make it easy to see," Katy Beth said. She closed the bottle and lowered it into the icy cold water.

"The hot water in this bottle acts just like a geyser," Katy Beth said. "It's a model of the geysers at Yellowstone National Park. When the hot water is released, it rushes to the top, like the steaming hot water coming up through Earth."

Katy Beth removed the lid from the bottle. The blue water rose quickly to the top, billowing out like a puff of smoke. Then it spread in a blue layer on top of the icy cold water.

"It looks like an underwater volcano!" Jeremy said.

Katy Beth smiled. She thought, *I DID IT! I made a volcano, too. And I'm the first one at the Science Fair to make* **this** *kind of volcano!*